I'M

JUST

SAYING!

I'M JUST SAYING!

PERSONAL QUOTATIONS, OPINIONATED ARTICLES, AND LIFE IN POETRY

EARL QUILLER

TABLE OF CONTENTS

PERSONAL QUOTATIONS

THESE QUOTATIONS ARE PERSONAL INSIGHTS ON THINGS HAPPENING IN OUR DAILY LIVES.

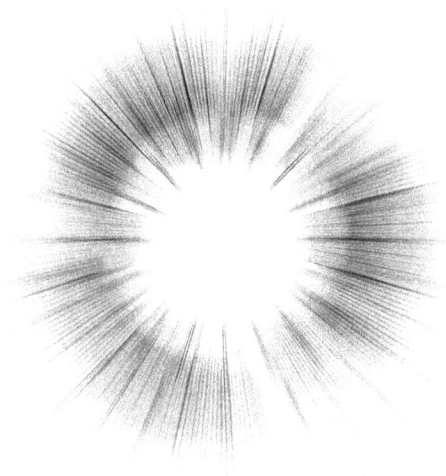

FRIENDSHIP SHINES A BRILLIANT GLEAM

OF HOPE INTO ONE'S LIFE.

SOMEBODY CARES.

BE PURPOSEFUL IN WHAT YOU SOW

THOSE THAT PLANT HATRED

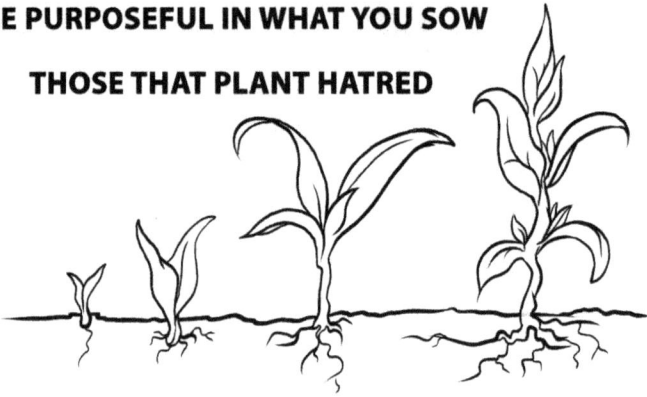

SHALL REAP DISCORD.

FAVOR ACCELERATES YOUR JOURNEY.

HOLY BIBLE

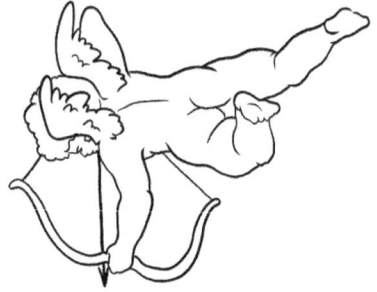

ONCE YOU FALL IN LOVE

THE OUTCOME CHANGES.

DON'T VOTE AND SURELY

YOUR VOTE WILL NOT COUNT.

THOUGHTS ARE PROOF
OF INWARD FEELINGS AND
ACTIONS PROVIDE OUTWARD CONSEQUENCES.

C Z S H N
O N V S R
K D V S R
Z K C S V
D V O H C
O H V C K
H Z C K O

WHEN OVERLY CRITICAL OF ANOTHER'S ACTION;

YOU BECOME BLIND TO YOUR ACTIONS.

PLACE YOUR HANDS ON YOUR CHEST.

THIS IS YOUR PURPOSE; SO LIVE IT.

THE STRONGEST PEOPLE ARE THE ONES THAT
FEEL PAIN, LOVE BEYOND ALL FAULTS, CRY WITHIN,
FIGHT BATTLES OF THE MIND AND STILL REMAIN SANE.

TRUST IS AN EMINENT
PART OF LOVE.

A HOPELESS INDIVIDUAL
IS A HELPLESS INDIVIDUAL.

NO GIFT IS ACCEPTABLE TO GOD UNTIL

WE HAVE GIVEN HIM OUR HEARTS;

FIRST THINGS FIRST.

**GOD HAS A BLESSING
FOR YOU.
BECOME UNSELFISHLY OBEDIENT.**

**SUCCESS IS
DETERMINATION
AND
NOT
DESTINATION.**

**IF YOU DO NOT
KNOW HOW TO DEAL WITH ME
THEN YOU DON'T KNOW ME.**

ACCEPT THE PAST,
EMBRACE THE FUTURE
AND LIVE IN THE PRESENT.

DON'T WORRY ABOUT
WHAT PEOPLE
DO
TO YOU; WORRY ABOUT
WHAT YOU
DO TO PEOPLE.

BY CHOICE WE AS
A PEOPLE HAVE BEEN BLIND TOO
LONG. OPEN YOUR EYES
A CHANGE IS WITHIN YOUR REACH.

**THE SMOG
OF INJUSTICE IS BEING REPLACED BY
THE FRESH AIR OF VINDICATION.**

LIVING FAITH

IS

FULFILLMENT,

BUT,

PATIENCE

IS

A VIRTUE.

**GENTRIFICATION AND SEGREGATION
ARE TWO WINGS
OF THE SAME BIRD.**

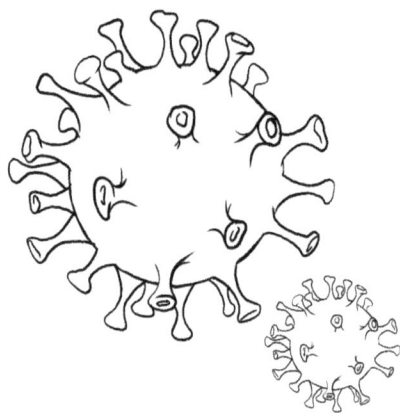

EVERY VIRUS RUNS OUT OF VICTIMS WHEN NO ONE IS LEFT.

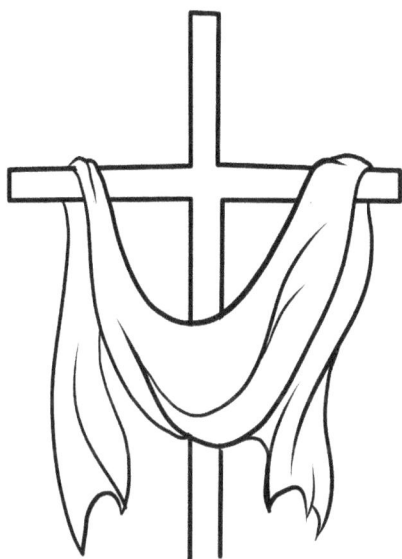

I AM BECAUSE GOD IS.

LOVE IS ... SOMETHING THAT LIVES IN
THE MIND AND LINGERS IN THE HEART

AS CLOSE AS GRANDUER IS TO DUST
AND GOD IS TO MAN.

IF LIFE IS FOR

THE LIVING, WHY ARE YOU

LOOKING FOR A WAY OUT.

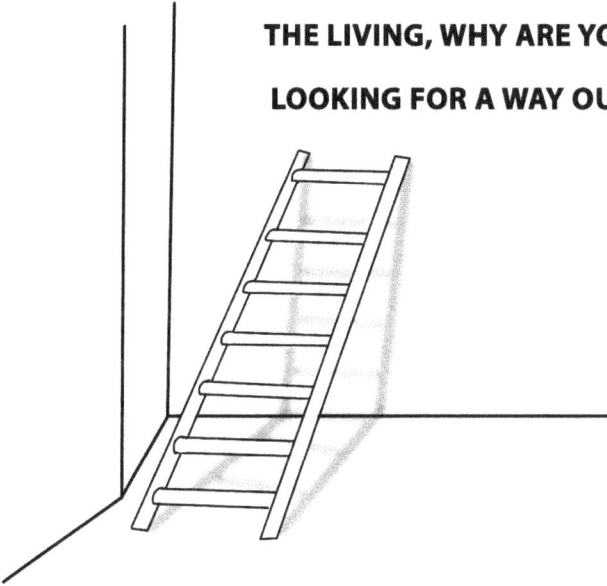

LOVE IS ... THE ESSENCE OF ALL THINGS THAT

ENCOMPASSES A TRUE RELATIONSHIP.

OUR ANALYTICAL THINKING

REDUCES OUR RELIGIOUS BELIEFS,

WITHOUT DIVINE INTERVENTION

WE CANNOT SAVE OURSELVES.

IN ORDER TO RESCUE OUR PEOPLE
FROM THE DIVISION OF DISPARITY.
WE MUST BRING FORTH THE GHOST
OF EQUALITY.

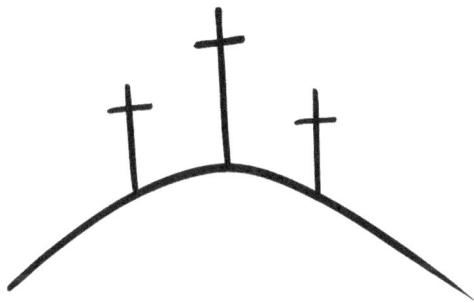

GOD IS BIGGER THAN ANY PROBLEM, BUT,
HOW GREAT IS THOU FAITH.

WE ARE IN THIS WORLD TOGETHER AND EACH DEATH

AFFECTS ALL OF US. EVERY FUNERAL BELL TOLLS FOR THEE.

THE PENALTY OF RACISM IS THE LOSS OF CULTURAL KNOWLEDGE.

THE WINDOWS OF TIME

ARE OBSCURE. TO SEE

CLEARLY YOU MUST THINK CLEARLY.

KEEP CHRIST IN CHRISTMAS AND GOD IN YOUR HEART.

LIFE IS
A GIFT
WHY ARE
YOU WAITING.

IF YOU THINK THAT YOU
HAVE COMPLETE CONTROL OF YOUR LIFE.
IT IS SELF-DECEPTION.

NOTHING IS
MORE MIND BOGGLING THAN
TRYING TO REACH THE LOST.

FAMILIES SHOULD LOVE ONE ANOTHER
AND NOT BE CONFRONTATIONAL.
AFTER ALL IS SAID AND DONE
WE ARE STILL AKIN.

**THE EPEDEMIC OF INJUSTICE AND
THE FATIGUE OF THIS NATION HAS AWAKENED
THE PEOPLE TO THE PROBLEMS OF AMERICA.**

ONE HAND WASHES
THE OTHER
AND BOTH
WASH THE FACE.

LOVE IS....

THE HAPPINESS OF THINGS WANTED

AND THE....

DREAMS OF THINGS THAT READILY EXIST.

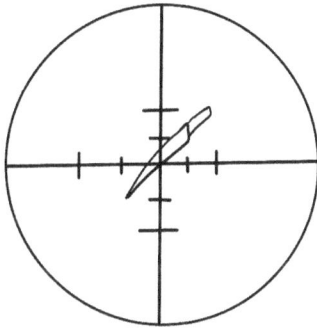

UNTIL THE RABBIT ARMS HIMSELF

HE WILL ALWAYS BE AT A DISADVANTAGE.

IF THERE
ARE TWO PEOPLE
IN A RACE
THERE IS
NO SECOND PLACE.

ALL PEOPLE ARE LIVING HISTORIES. HISTORY
IS THE BRIDGE FROM THE PAST TO THE PRESENT.
UNDERSTANDING THE CONNECTION BETWEEN THE PAST
AND THE PRESENT IS A CATALYST FOR UNDERSTANDING
THE
CONDITION OF BEING HUMAN. SOME OF US SPEAK A
DIALECT
FROM THE PAST; IS THIS NOT A LIVING HISTORY?

THE CORE WORD IS THANKS

(GIVING THANKS FOR WHAT YOU ARE GRATEFUL FOR).

TO WHOM MUCH IS GIVEN

MUCH WILL BE REQUIRED. (LUKE 12:48)

**YOU CAN'T GET LOST
ON A ROAD THAT LEADS
TO NOWHERE.**

BEING WORTHY, KNOWING, DESERVING, AND
DEMANDING TO BE TREATED RIGHT IS SELF- RESPECT
DO NOT TOLERATE ANYTHING ELSE.

IT IS NO MYSTERY WHY
YOU ARE BEING TREATED THIS WAY.
THIS IS HOW THEY FEEL ABOUT YOU.

WHEN SOMEONE WALKS OUT OF YOUR LIFE LET
THEM GO. REMEMBER THEY ARE LEAVING YOU. IF THEY
ARE NOT WITH YOU THEN THEY MUST BE AGAINST YOU.

October 2021

					1	2
3	4	5	6	7	8	9
10					15	16
17					22	23
24	25	26	27	28	29	30
31						

WHAT IS LIFE? IS IT THE TIME SPENT HERE ON EARTH, IS IT THE BEAT OF YOUR HEART OR IS IT YOUR SOUL LEAVING YOUR BODY AT DEATH.

JUDGMENTAL PERCEPTIONS WILL CREATE FAKE
ASSUMPTIONS. ONE SHOULD COMPARE PERSONAL
EXPERIENCES TO THE EXPERIENCES OF OTHERS.

YOU CAN DEVIATE FROM
THE FACTS, BUT,
YOU CAN'T HIDE THE TRUTH.
HIS - STORY.

LIFE MAKES YOU FEEL
LIKE DAY BREAKING INTO NIGHT. WHICH HAPPENS
SO SWIFT; YOU WILL NEVER KNOW
WHAT TIME IT HAS TAKEN PLACE.

LIFE IS LIKE A VAPOR.
HERE FOR A LITTLE WHILE THEN
VANISHES INTO OBSCURITY.

LOVE IS ... AN OVER ANXIETY OF

EMOTIONS WHICH FOREVER

FLOWS LIKE AN ENDLESS STREAM.

LOVE IS THE HAPPINESS
OF THINGS WANTED AND THE DREAMS
OF THINGS SURREAL.

**YOUR ENVIRONMENT IS A
CATALYST TO YOUR DRAMA; CHANGE
AND REALIZE THE DIFFERENCE.**

NO ONE SHOULD CONSIDER
THEMSELVES ISOLATED. EVERYONE
IS A PART OF THE MAIN FRAME
OF ECONOMIC DEVELOPMENT.

OPINIONATED ARTICLES

THESE ARTICLES ARE MY PERSONAL OPINIONS ABOUT HAPPENINGS IN MY ENVIRONMENT. THEY ARE NOT THE VIEWS OF THE PUBLISHER.

JESUS PAID IT ALL

PLAUSIBLE DENIABILITY IS THE ABILITY FOR PERSONS TO DENY KNOWLEDGE OF OR RESPONSIBILITY FOR ANY DAMNABLE ACTIONS COMMITTED BY OTHERS. LACK OF EVIDENCE CANNOT CONFIRM THEIR PARTICIPATION. OFFICIALS MAY DENY ANY AWARENESS OF ANY ACT OR WRONGDOING. BUT THE LACK OF THIS EVIDENCE TO THE CONTRARY MAKES THE DENIAL PLAUSIBLE; THAT IS CREDIBLE. IT MAKES IT UNACTIONIONABLE SHIFTING THE BLAME TO OTHERS WITH HOPE THAT PEOPLE WILL NOT FIND THE TRUTH. IN SOME ORGANIZATIONS COMMAND RESPONSIBILITY EXIST TO HOLD THOSE INVOLVED RESPONSIBLE. DENIAL OF THEIR INVOLVEMENT WOULD BE NULLIFIED. PLAUSIBLE DENIABILITY REFERS TO LACK OF EVIDENCE PROVING AN ALLEGATION. STANDARDS OF PROOF VARY IN CIVIL AND CRIMINAL CASES. IN CIVIL CASES, THE STANDARD OF PROOF IS "PREPONDERANCE OF THE EVIDENCE" WHEREAS IN A CRIMINAL MATTER, THE STANDARD IS "BEYOND A REASONABLE DOUBT." IF AN OPPONENT CANNOT PROVIDE EVIDENCE FOR HIS ALLEGATION; ONE CAN PLAUSIBLY DENY THE ALLEGATION EVEN THOUGH IT MAY BE TRUE.

LOVE IS...

Regardless of what you do, continue to do or say, love don't love nobody. Love is the most profound emotion known to man. It is a force of nature. We cannot command or demand love from another. Love is not the person it is the reciprocal feeling between people. In essence love does not love you, if you don't love yourself. How can you recognize that feeling when you have never realized the greatness of it? Love does not mean being a charity for someone but being a meaningful element in someone's life. Providing them with a profound source of fulfillment. It is an object of thought to be known only by the intellect.

ENOUGH IS ENOUGH

IT IS REALLY A TOXIC SITUATION AS TO WHY BLACKS ARE KILLING ONE ANOTHER. I WOULD HATE TO SAY, "IT IS MOSTLY GANG RELATED." THERE IS A HIGH UNEMPLOYMENT RATE FOR BLACKS IN OUR AREA. IN ADDITION, THE POLICE VIEW US AS NUMBERS, STATISTICS AND DISPENSABLE. YOUNG BLACKS ARE RUNNING AROUND UNEDUCATED, UNINFORMED, AND THEY HAVE ALL THE ANSWERS. THE STREETS OF RALEIGH ARE FLOWING WITH THE BLOOD OF OUR YOUNG BLACK MEN. AS CITIZENS OF THIS CITY WE SHOULD SAY, "ENOUGH IS ENOUGH." IT IS TIME FOR US TO DO SOMETHING TO ALLEVIATE THIS PROBLEM. YOUNG BLACKS SHOULD STOP HOLDING GRUDGES, HATING EACH OTHER AND TAKE ON THE MESSAGE OF JESUS. THIS WILL ENABLE THEM TO MAKE A DIFFERENCE IN THEIR LIVES AND IN THE LIVES OF OTHERS. IF BLACK LIVES MATTER, THEN JESUS SHOULD MATTER (BE THE DRIVING FORCE) IN BLACK LIVES. WE SHOULD STOP ASSIGNING OURSELVES GHETTO NAMES AND REPUTATIONS. JUST BECAUSE YOUR NICKNAME IS BLOCKBUSTER DOES NOT MEAN THAT YOU ARE THE BIGGEST FOOL ON THE BLOCK.

WE NEED TO LOOK AT THE WAY GUNS AND DRUGS ARE GETTING INTO OUR COMMUNITIES. OUR YOUNG PEOPLE HAVE LOST HOPE. THEY TEND TO THINK THAT VIOLENCE IS THEIR REWARD OR PENALTY FOR BEING WRONGED. GRANDMA USE TO SAY, "YOU CAN CATCH MORE FLIES WITH SUGAR THAN YOU CAN WITH STINK. LOOK INTO YOUR SITUATION BEFORE IT IS TOO LATE. YOU ARE A SYSTEMIC PROBLEM AND BEING INSTITUTIONALIZED IS NOT GOING TO HELP. ENOUGH IS ENOUGH.

BEING A CHRISTIAN

This is a reminder that all of us are human beings. You have admitted that you had an oversight. The Life of a Godly person is an example of the body of Christ. It depends on our moral character, and it means a lot to the spirit. It is not what we say, but what we do. How we live, how we love, and how we serve plays a dominant role. With Jesus on the inside, we possess the character of the Holy Ghost. At this moment you have come to the conclusion as to what went wrong. Self-control is one of the greatest attributes of anyone that has received, the power of the Holy Spirit Continue to do God's. Work and may God bless you." The Spirit of the Lord God is upon me; because the Lord hath anointed me to preach good tidings unto the meek; he hath sent me to bind up the brokenhearted, to proclaim liberty to the captives' and the opening of the prisons to them that are bound." (Isaiah 61:1)

JOB SECURITY

The hiring of non-career employees has a lot to do with the demise of the USPS. If you do not have pride in your uniform, then you won't have pride in your work. Your salary is what you get for doing a days' work for a days' pay. It is not how much you can get paid in two weeks to pay your bills or etc. Knowing how to manage your money has a lot to do with managing your time on the clock. Productivity declines with attitudes, job assignments, knowing your assignment, servicing the public and morale. The USPS profits come from service and selling postage. Service is the number one product. USPS needs to put a stamp on the service and put that in the mail to be delivered. Being a dysfunctional place to work is because the USPS is not functioning to its' utmost ability. Management can share the blame as well as lower-level employees. All involved should think of this as being their business and work together to come to a common goal. That goal should be to do their job in the most efficient manner possible. The union should stop blaming management and vice versa. When the doors of the plant are closed who is going to take the blame? Now is the time to work in unison. Everyone on the clock will get paid; so, all should come together to improve our NUMBERS.

DOING YOUR BEST

SOME ORGANIZATIONS THINK THAT GETTING PAID WELL IS A SELF-MOTIVATING INCENTIVE. INCLUDED IN THIS INCENTIVE YOU WILL BE EMPOWERED, INVOLVED, TRUSTED, CHALLENGED, AND ON A MISSION. PROMOTIONS ARE INDIVIDUAL CHALLENGES. IN ORDER TO HAVE KNOWLEDGEABLE EMPLOYEES; THEY MUST BE TRAINED. THEN YOU WILL HEAR, "I DON'T GET PAID TO DO THAT." IF YOU VALUE YOUR FELLOW EMPLOYEE RELATIONSHIP; YOU WILL HELP TRAIN THEM TO DO THEIR JOB CORRECT.

ARE YOU VALUED? YES, FOR SOME CUSTOMERS THINK VERY HIGHLY OF THEIR MAIL CARRIER. YOUR VALUE AS A MAIL CARRIER IS A COMMUNAL BEING OF THE COMMUNITY OR PUBLIC. YOU ARE APPRECIATED WHEN YOU SUCCEED, IF NOT BY MANAGEMENT, YOUR CUSTOMERS OR YOUR FAMILY. NOW THE PERCENTAGE HAS BEEN CHALLENGED. EACH EMPLOYEE HAS THEIR OWN STATS. SOME CARE AND SOME DO NOT CARE. I HAVE ALWAYS HAD THIS SAYING, "A CREATURE OF BAD HABITS; BAD THINGS HAPPEN TO THEM."

RELIGION

YOU COULD HAVE TOLD HIM THAT HE WAS LIVING PROOF THAT THERE IS A GOD. BUT IT IS HARD TO TRY TO CONVINCE A NON¬BELIEVER. "YOU WILL SEEK ME AND FIND ME; WHEN YOU SEEK ME WITH ALL YOUR HEART, I WILL BE FOUND BY YOU." (JER. 29:12) YOU MAY NOT BE ABLE TO CONVINCE HIM IN ONE HOUR, ONE DAY OR MAYBE ONE YEAR. BUT IF YOU LEAD HIM TO THE TABLE AND IF HE IS REALLY HUNGRY, HE WILL EAT. YOUR OPINION DOES NOT MEAN ANYTHING TO SOME PEOPLE. THEY WILL HAVE TO COME UP WITH THE IDEA THEMSELVES. YOU COULD PROBABLY SAY, " TAKE THIS BIBLE HOME AND READ JEREMIAH 12TH CHAPTER; COME BACK TUESDAY NIGHT AND LET'S DISCUSS IT. LET HIM RELATE TO THE SUBJECT OF RELIGION RATHER THAN TRY TO TELL HIM STRAIGHT OUT. MAYBE HE WILL OPEN HIS HEART AND FIND GOD.

RIGHTEOUSNESS

WE THAT ARE STRONG OUGHT TO BEAR THE INFIRMITIES OF THE WEAK AND NOT PLEASE OURSELVES. (ROMAN 15:1) SOME INDIVIDUALS ARE WEAK AND WE SHOULD BE SUPPORTIVE OF THEIR SITUATION. FOR ALL HAVE SINNED AND COME SHORT OF THE GLORY OF GOD. WE TEND TO LOOK DOWN ON THEM AND PASS JUDGMENT ON THEIR WAYS AND OPINIONS. WE HAVE GIVEN MAN'S LAW APPROVAL OVER GOD'S LAW. YOU ARE JUSTIFIED BY REACHING OUT TO THOSE THAT NEED HELP.

JUSTIFICATION=GLORIFICATION=SANTIFICATION. YOU HAVE PUT YOUR FAITH BEFORE EVERYTHING ELSE. THROUGH GOD'S GRACE AND MERCY, YOU SHALL BE REWARDED. IT IS BECAUSE OF GOD'S UNMERITED FAVOR THAT HUMAN BEINGS CAN BE DECLARED RIGHTEOUS BEFORE GOD.

A TIME OF PRAYER

DEAR WATCHFUL AND CARING GOD; GIVE US THE INTENTIONALITY TO EXPERIENCE YOUR WONDERFUL BLESSINGS. LORD, GIVE US THE WILL TO TAKE TIME FROM OUR BUSY DAY TO BE WITH YOU. GOD, BLESS AMERICA AND THE PEOPLE THAT ARE TRYING TO RETURN HOME FROM VARIOUS TRIPS. "NOT THAT WE ARE SUFFICIENT OF OUR SELVES TO THINK ANYTHING AS OF OURSELVES; BUT OUR SUFFICIENCY IS OF GOD; WHO ALSO HATH MADE US ABLE MINISTERS OF THE NEW TESTAMENT; NOT OF THE LETTER, BUT OF THE SPIRIT; FOR THE LETTER KILLETH, BUT THE SPIRIT GIVETH LIFE." (2 COR. 3:5-6)

TRUST GOD

"WHILE WE LOOK NOT AT THE THINGS WHICH ARE SEEN, BUT ON WHAT IS UNSEEN, SINCE WHAT IS SEEN IS TEMPORARY BUT, WHAT IS UNSEEN IS ETERNAL" (2 COR. 4:17-18) IN OTHER WORDS ALL CONDITIONS POSITIVE OR NEGATIVE ARE TEMPORARY. WHETHER IT IS GOOD OR BAD. LIFE IS A CRAZY NOT FEEL. BAD THINGS DO HAPPEN AND HOW YOU RESPOND TO THEM DEFINES YOUR CHARACTER AND QUALITY OF LIFE. NOW, YOU CAN JUST SIT THERE (HAVE A PITY PARTY) OR YOU CAN TREASURE WHAT MATTERS THE MOST WHICH IS LIFE. GOD LETS EVERYTHING HAPPEN FOR A REASON. IT IS A PART OF THE LIFE CYCLE. THIS TOO SHALL PASS; GROW IN LIFE AND GET OVER IT.

IN THE SPIRIT

IF YOU DO NOT KNOW HOW GOOD THE LORD HAS BEEN TO YOU. THEN PRAYING IN THE SPIRITUAL REALM IS A GOOD START. YOU GOT TO HAVE A SPIRITUAL RELATIONSHIP WITH THE LORD. "AND WHATEVER YOU DO IN WORD OR DEED; DO EVERYTHING IN THE NAME OF THE LORD JESUS. GIVING THANKS TO GOD THE FATHER THROUGH HIM." (COL. 3:17) WHEN PRAYING IN THE SPIRITUAL REALM WHATEVER YOU ASK FOR, HE GIVES TO YOU IN YOUR SPIRIT FOR HIS SPIRIT. EVERY WORD OR DEED SHOULD BE IN THE NAME OF THE LORD. LET THE WORD OF GOD ENRICH YOUR WISDOM AND YOUR DAILY TEACHINGS.

BY CHOICE

WE WANT THE SAME THINGS IN LIFE AS OTHER PEOPLE OR RACES. SOME OF WHICH ARE FREEDOM, CRIME FREE STREETS, THE CHANCE FOR PROSPERITY, AS FEW PEOPLE SUFFERING AS POSSIBLE, HEALTHY CHILDREN, UNQUESTIONABLE BELIEF IN GOD, AND SAFE HAVENS TO CALL OUR HOMES. THE ARGUMENT IS HOW TO ACHIEVE THEM. LIBERALS BELIEVE IN GOVERNMENT ACTION TO ACHIEVE EQUAL OPPORTUNITY AND EQUALITY FOR ALL. CONSERVATIVES BELIEVE IN PERSONAL RESPONSIBILITY, LIMITED GOVERNMENT, FREE MARKETS, INDIVIDUAL LIBERTY, TRADITIONAL AMERICAN VALUES AND A STRONG NATIONAL DEFENSE. PROGRESSIVE BELIEVERS THINK THAT EVERYONE GETS A FAIR SHOT; IF EVERYONE DOES HIS OR HER FAIR SHARE, AND EVERYONE PLAYS BY THE SAME RULES. WHETHER YOU ARE A DEMOCRAT, REPUBLICAN, OR AN INDEPENDENT; YOU FIT SOMEWHERE IN THIS REALM. THIS IS JUST A SYNOPSIS TO ENLIGHTEN YOU AS TO WHERE YOU MIGHT FIT IN.

HE HAS THE KEYS

JESUS HAS RISEN AND WE AS HIS PEOPLE NEED TO TAKE ADVANTAGE OF THIS OCCASION. WE NEED THE SAME TYPE OF METAMORPHOSIS IN OUR LIVES AS IN THE INSECT WORLD. LIKE THE TRANSFORMATION OF A CATERPILLAR INTO A BUTTERFLY AND IN AMPHIBIANS, THE CHANGING OF A TADPOLE INTO A FROG. THE TRANSFORMATION OF THE HUMAN BODY IS LIKE A CHAMELEON. IT IS FITTING; LIKE A VIRUS IT IS CONTAGIOUS AND JUST LIKE AN INDIVIDUAL'S PERSONALITY IT IS CHANGEABLE. IF AT ANY POINT IN YOUR LIFE YOU WANTED TO MAKE A CHANGE; TODAY IS THE DAY.

YOUR TRANSFORMATION DOES NOT HAVE ANYTHING TO DO WITH WHAT OTHERS THINK. PEOPLE WILL ALWAYS HAVE THAT INTUITION ABOUT THEM. GOD LOVES YOU AND HE WANTS YOU TO BE HAPPY, YOU HAVE NOT BECAUSE YOU ASK NOT. JESUS' RESURRECTION MAKES US MORE THAN CONQUERORS. " DON'T COPY THE BEHAVIOR AND CUSTOMS OF THIS WORLD, BUT LET GOD TRANSFORM YOU INTO A NEW PERSON BY CHANGING THE WAY YOU THINK. THEN YOU WILL LEARN TO KNOW GOD'S WILL FOR YOU, WHICH IS GOOD, PLEASING AND PERFECT. " (ROMANS 12:2 NLT)

HE HAS RISEN

AGAINST HOPELESSNESS AND DESPAIR WHO WILL ROLL THE STONE AWAY FOR US. WE KNOW THAT GOD LIVES, SO, WE TOO LIVE. ANYONE THAT ACCEPTS THE COMFORTS OF CHRIST CAN FACE THE OBSTACLES OF LIFE, WE CAN DO ALL THINGS THROUGH CHRIST THAT STRENGTHENS. CHRIST WILL DO FOR US WHEN WE CAN'T DO FOR OURSELVES. THE REASON MANY CHRISTIANS ARE LEADING SUCH DEFEATED LIVES; THEY DON'T KNOW THEIR POSITION IN LIFE. IF YOU DON'T KNOW WHO YOU ARE; YOU ARE PRIME CANDIDATE FOR DEFEAT. WHILE YOU ARE OUT THERE JUST FLOATING ALONG; THE WAVES OF LIFE WILL WASH YOU UNDER. YOU NEED TO KNOW WHO YOU ARE AND CONNECT TO THE FATHER, SON AND HOLY SPIRIT. WHEN YOU KNOW WHO YOU ARE; YOU WILL HAVE PEACE AND JOY "YE ARE LITTLE CHILDREN AND HAVE OVERCOME THEM: BECAUSE GREATER IS HE THAT IS IN YOU; THAN HE THAT IS IN THE WORLD." (1 JOHN 4:4)

MIND CONTROL

Sometimes we have to find out where we are in life. Whether it is our choices, a lesson, a reflection, or just pain period. Our vision alone recognizes the problem and has a tendency to guide us away from our dilemma. Certainly, we don't want this to be a whole life experience. By using a scientific process called inductive and deductive reasoning we can get a valid explanation.

JESUS WILL MAKE AWAY

WE as Christians should start each day with a thankful heart. Regardless of our situation the Lord will make a way out of no way. In the face of adversity God will fix what is broken, replenish what is gone, restore calm during storms in our lives, and most of all He is the Alpha and the Omega; the 'beginning and the end. Have faith, another day another blessing. Remember you didn't wake up this morning on your own. Never forget that on your best day God was overshadowing your actions "He that followeth after righteousness and mercy findeth life, righteousness, and honour. (Proverbs 21:21)

REASONS

People are marching against idealism, social injustice, police violations, deaths of blacks in police custody, etc. It would be wrong to think that these protestors do not have substantial issues. It really becomes a concern when all of the community blends together to protest about the same systemic problems. Sure, there are going to be people that want to profit from the protest by creating a riot of sorts. But be mindful that your protest is centered on non-violence and not by any means necessary. This systematic oppression of black people has run its' course. The only limits that we have in life are our choices. A great change is about to be birthed in America. We as people of color should be receptive of these changes. This is America, the land of the free and the home of the brave. "Think not that I come to destroy the law, or the prophets: I am not to destroy, but to fulfill." (Matthew 5:17)

FEAR (Face Everything and Rise)

Face everything and rise the choice is yours. This fear lives in the minds of people. They seem to be threatened by what the rabbit would do if he had the gun. We have been dealing with these racial tensions for many years. "Black Lives Matter"; is a slogan to pinpoint the indifferences that we have suffered. There is a remedy for this fear: (a) We must acknowledge the existence of all our problems, (b) We must restore a friendly relationship between all races, (c) We must make permanent changes to this racial tension in order to improve it. (d) We must establish a bond of communications, feelings, pride, and emotions. By sitting back and doing nothing we have become complicit in our own situation. This new generation is about justice for everyone and not JUST-US. (a) Recognize (b) Reconcile (c) Reform (d) Reconnect

BEAUTY

A LONG TIME AGO I WAS TOLD; "BEAUTY IS IN THE EYES OF THE BEHOLDER." IT IS WHAT AN INDIVIDUAL SEES EXTERNALLY. A PRETTY FACE CAN ATTRACT PEOPLE WITHOUT DOING ANYTHING SPECIAL. BUT A PERSON WITH INTERNAL BEAUTY HAS A GOD GIVEN ABILITY TO DEVELOP STRONG AND ENDURING RELATIONSHIPS. THEY HAVE A LOT OF GOOD CHARACTERISTICS SUCH AS HONESTY, CONFIDENCE, TOLERANCE, KINDNESS, RESPECT AND STRONG MORAL VALUES. TO SAY; "BEAUTY IS ONLY SKIN DEEP IS JUST SCRATCHING THE SURFACE."

BEING SAVED

It seems to be very unbiblical to say that we are saved by cooperating with God by doing good works. A person is justified by faith (Roman. 5: I). It was Jesus' death on the cross and subsequent resurrection that achieved our salvation. We are saved from God's judgment of sin. Our sin has separated us from God and the consequence of sin is death. Jesus equated being saved with entering the kingdom of God. (Matt. 19:24-25) The bible tells us in so many words that if we claim to be Christian and we do not have good works, ,then we are not saved.(1John 2:4) Furthermore the bible says once we are saved, we are not free to do unsavory things (Rom. 6:1-2) Our works, our good deeds, have no effect upon our salvation. We are obligated to God to be good. (Jn. 14:15) This conversation can continue to include Repentance, Will, Pardon and Forgiving of Sin, and once again Our Divine Gift.

THE DOCTRINE

The Doctrine of Salvation is the belief that an individual is in some danger from which they must be saved. Christians believe that the danger is spiritually centered in each person's soul and pertains mainly to life after death. If a person is saved, they will live in eternal happiness; if not they will live in "wrath", that is God's judgment of sin. Sure, an individual can listen, dance, sing, and enjoy secular music.

Everything is surrounded by the lyrics, style, it's purpose and is it praiseworthy. You would not consider yourself a Christian and you are dancing provocatively. The question is; is it a sin to listen, enjoy, dance and sing along with secular music?

INQUISITIVE

People interpret the bible to their advantage. "Wives, submit yourselves unto your husbands, as it is fit in the Lord" (Col. 3:18) People will turn their relationship around with this verse, but now read the next verse. "Husbands, love your wives, and be not bitter against them." (Col.3:19) If you are going to speak on part of it speak on all of it. You either believe in all the bible or none of it. Don't pick and choose verses that suits the situation.

DREAMS TO REMEMBER!!!!!!

All of us have dreams here in America. Ronald Reagan's dream was a city on a hill, John F. Kennedy's dream was what we could do for our country, and Dr. Martin L. King's dream was racial equality. I ask you; what is your dream? America has faced many adversaries through wars and military conflicts. It is now time for us to come to the aid of our people. We are culturally connected regardless.

It is really a toxic situation as to why blacks are killing one another. I would hate to say, "it is mostly gang related." There is a high unemployment rate for blacks in our area. In addition, young blacks are running around uneducated, and they have all the answers. It is time for us to do something to alleviate this problem.

We that are strong ought to bear the infirmities of the weak and not please ourselves. (Romans 15:1) Being that individuals are weak we should he supportive of their situation. We have given man's law approval over God's law. We are justified by reaching out to those that need help and through God's grace and mercy we shall be rewarded.

The life of a godly person is an example of the body of Christ. It depends on our moral character, and it means a lot to the spirit. It Is not what we say, but what we do, how we live, how we love, and how we serve plays a dominant role.

Sometimes we have to find out where we are in life. Whether it is our choices, a lesson, a reflection or just pain period. Our vision alone recognizes the problem and has a tendency to guide us away from our dilemma. Open your eyes the time is NOW.

NO WORRIES

THE DEVIL'S MAIN FOCUS IS TO THWART, DISTRACT, DIVERT AND DISARM THE SERVANTS OF GOD. THE PEOPLE THAT ARE PROMOTING THE RULES AND PROMISES OF GOD ON EARTH. WHY SHOULD HE ATTACK SOMEONE ALREADY IN HIS GRIP? HE WILL FOCUS HIS ATTENTION ON THOSE WHO ARE THE BIGGEST THREAT TO HIS DESIRES. REMEMBER HE IS IN A POWER GRAB WITH GOD. IN OTHER WORDS, IF YOU ARE AN ATHEIST (DOES NOT BELIEVE IN THE EXISTENCE OF GOD) THEN YOU HAVE NO PROBLEM BECAUSE YOU ARE NO CHALLENGE.

MY PRAYER

Oh, heavenly Father we are most thankful for all you have done including waking us this morning. We recognize that you are the Alpha and Omega. You are the beginning and the end, from everlasting to everlasting. We would like to praise you for your goodness, mercy, power, and your love. There is no one in the world to compare to you. Who else will protect all kinds of people? Lord, we confess at times we have fallen short. But forgive and cleanse us for our wrong doings; oh Lord. Lord, we are trying to be faithful servants of your word. A branch cannot bear fruit when severed from the vine. We cannot bear fruit when separated from you. Lord, we would like to thank you for the many blessings bestowed upon us. We give thanks to you for your love. Lord, your faithfulness and love live forever. We would like for you to be a beacon in our daily lives and activities. Lord: bless the sick, those confined, the homeless, the haves, the have nots, those that are here and those that are waiting on your final judgment. Lord, lead us and guide us so that we can become better stewards. Draw us closer Lord; so that our relationship will grow stronger. Lord, give us the inspiration to see in others what we see in you. In Jesus name I pray. Amen.

PURPOSE DRIVEN WOMAN

IF YOU ARE A PURPOSE DRIVEN WOMAN. THEN GOD'S PURPOSE IS YOUR PURPOSE. YOU DO NOT NEED ANYONE TO DISCOVER YOU WHEN YOU HAVE GOD. IF YOU ARE STRUGGLING WITH A SITUATION; GIVE IT TO GOD. SOME OF YOU HAVE A POOR CONCEPT OF YOURSELVES AND OTHERS HAVE INHERITED FEELINGS WHICH BRING ABOUT LOW SELF-ESTEEM. I WILL TELL YOU THERE IS SO MUCH GREATNESS IN YOU. GOD MADE YOU JUST THE WAY HE WANTED YOU TO BE. RAISE YOURS HANDS TO THE HEAVENS; FOR YOUR HELP COMES FROM THE LORD. IF YOU ARE GOING TO REIGN WITH GOD; YOU WILL HAVE TO FEEL THE SPIRIT OF GOD. YOU NEED TO KNOW AND BELIEVE WHO YOU ARE IN CHRIST. BE A PECULIAR PERSON; YOU ARE THE LIGHT OF THE WORLD AND THE SALT OF THE EARTH. YOUR WALK SHOULD BE THE SAME AS YOUR TALK.

WHAT'S LOVE GOT TO DO WITH IT

WHEN WE HEAR THE WORD "LOVE"; WE AUTOMATICALLY THINK OF A ROMANTIC KIND OF LOVE. LOVING SOMEONE IN BIBLICAL TERMS IS AGAPE LOVE. AGAPE LOVE IS THE HIGHEST FORM OF LOVE; THE LOVE OF GOD FOR MAN AND OF MAN FOR GOD. DON'T BE CONFUSED WITH "PHILEO" (BROTHERLY LOVE). MANY TIMES, IN THE BIBLE JESUS COMMANDS US TO LOVE ONE ANOTHER. JESUS SAITH UNTO HIM, "THOU SHALT LOVE THE LORD THY GOD WITH ALL THY HEART, AND WITH ALL THY SOUL, AND WITH ALL THY MIND." (MT. 22:37) THIS WAS THE MOST IMPORTANT COMMANDMENT; THE SECOND; WAS TO LOVE YOUR NEIGHBOR AS YOURSELF. YOUR NEIGHBOR ENCOMPASSES YOUR CO-WORKERS, CLASSMATES, ANYONE AROUND YOU# YOUR ACTUAL NEIGHBORS, ETC. SURELY IF GOD LOVED US; WE SHOULD LOVE ONE ANOTHER. HOW CAN YOU SAY, "I LOVE GOD BUT I HATE MY BROTHER? " IF WE CAN'T LOVE THE PEOPLE THAT WE CAN SEE; HOW CAN WE LOVE GOD WHOM WE CANNOT SEE? LOVING GOD AND LOVING PEOPLE; THE TWO GO TOGETHER LIKE HUSBAND AND WIFE. WE ARE INSULTING GOD'S CREATION WHEN WE SAY, "WE HATE." AS CHRISTIANS WE MUST LOVE ALL PEOPLE. WE MUST REMEMBER THAT WE ARE NO LONGER LIKE PEOPLE OF THE WORLD OR DESIRE THE THINGS OF IT. INSTEAD WE OUGHT TO BE CHRIST LIKE, SO, WHEN PEOPLE SEE US, THEY WILL ULTIMATELY SEE SUCH.

LIFE IN POETRY

THESE POEMS ARE ABOUT THE TRIALS AND TRIBULATIONS OF LIFE

I SIT IN DARKNESS

     I SIT IN DARKNESS ALL ALONE
JUST A LONELY MAN IN AN EMPTY HOME.
WAITING AND HOPING FOR ANOTHER DAY
TO SIT AT HOME; HOPE AND PRAY.
THAT ONE DAY SHE WILL RETURN TO ME
AND UNCHAIN THIS DARKNESS AND SET ME FREE.
TO ROAM AMONGST THE BEST OF MANKIND
TO FEEL FREE AND CHANGE MY MIND.
ABOUT EVERYTHING IN LIFE ON A WHOLE
TO SATISFY MY CONSCIENCE AND REGAIN MY SOUL.
     I SIT IN DARKNESS FAR AND NEAR
TRYING TO FORGET MY LOVE SO DEAR.
THAT I GAVE EVERYTHING FOR GRANTED
SHE LEFT ME ALONE AND SO ENCHANTED.
ABOUT THE LOVE I THOUGHT WAS THERE
I HARDLY HAD ENOUGH CLOTHES TO WEAR.
     I SIT IN DARKNESS FEELING GOOD AND MILD
I KNOW THAT I WILL BE HERE FOR A WHILE.
I TRIED TO THINK AND OFTEN TRY
TO SIT IN DARKNESS AND DO NOT CRY.
FOR DARKNESS IS A VERY BAD THING
IT WILL MAKE YOU SAD AND MAKE YOU SING
     I SIT IN DARKNESS AND I MUST SAY
THAT DARKNESS IS A VERY BAD WAY.
TO SPEND MY
LIFE IN THIS WORLD
WITHOUT HOPE OF SEEING MY GIRL.

AND THAT IS A MESS

SO, I GUESS I'LL JUST SIT IN DARKNESS.

I HAVE LIVED MY LIFE

I HAVE LIVED MY LIFE WITH HATE AND DISGRACE
FOR THERE WERE MANY PROBLEMS I HAD TO FACE.
IN THIS CRUEL WORLD FAST AND ALIVE
A TIMID MIND CANNOT SURVIVE.
BEING ONE OF MANY WHO LOST THEIR LOVE
I LIVED MY LIFE ON THE WINGS OF A DOVE.
I TRIED TO FLY TO SOME SECLUDED PLACE
BUT NEVER THE LEAST I COULDN'T HIDE MY FACE.
I HAVE LIVED MY LIFE WITH PARTIES AND WHISKEY
AND MET LOTS OF GIRLS BOTH YOUNG AND FRISKY.
NONE OF WHOM EVEN CROSSED MY MIND
FOR I HAVE LIVED THE BEST OF MY LIFE THIS DAY AND TIME.
I HAD SOME BAD DAYS AND NIGHTS
I HAVE STRUGGLED HARD TO SURVIVE AND LOTS OF FIGHTS.
ALTHOUGH I HAVE BEEN UP AND DOWN
THE BEST DAYS OF MY LIFE WERE DOWN HERE ON THE GROUND.
I HAVE LIVED MY LIFE WITH HUNGER AND GREED
TO SOME I SAY PLEASE TAKE HEED.
LIFE IS A FUNNY THING YOU KNOW
IT KEEPS YOU RUNNING AND ON THE GO.
THE BEST THINGS IN LIFE ARE HARD TO REVIVE
SO DO THE BEST YOU CAN TO SURVIVE
FOR I HAVE LIVED MY LIFE.

DIDN'T YOU KNOW

DIDN'T YOU KNOW THAT LIFE WAS A DRAG
FOR IT HAS ME IN THE SAME OLD BAG.
THINGS IN LIFE ARE HARD TO CONCEIVE
FOR IT IS BETTER TO GIVE THAN TO RECEIVE.
WHAT HAS LIFE DONE FOR YOU
BUT MADE YOU MISERABLE AND FEELING BLUE,
FOR THE STRONG IN LIFE HAS TO SURVIVE
AND THE WEAK SHALL FALL BY THE WAYSIDE.
DIDN'T YOU KNOW THAT SOME THINGS ARE FUNNY
WHEN YOU GO OUT AND SPEND ALL YOUR MONEY.
ON SOMETHING THAT IS NOT WORTH A DIME
FOR IT IS JUST A WASTE OF PRECIOUS TIME.
PEOPLE THINK THAT THEY CAN GET BY
SOBBING LONG AND TRYING TO CRY.
ABOUT THE THINGS THAT THEY HAD LOST
UNWILLING AND UNABLE TO PAY THE COST.
DIDN'T YOU KNOW THAT YOUR LOVE HAS GONE
AND LEFT YOU SITTING ALL ALONE.
TO THINK ABOUT THE TIMES, YOU HAD
SOME WERE GOOD AND OTHERS WERE BAD.
BUT THE BEST THING IN LIFE IS HAPPINESS
WITHOUT IT YOU ARE MISERABLE AND IN A MESS.
FOR HAPPINESS WILL MAKE YOU GLOW
AND YOU CAN SAY TO YOURSELF I DIDN'T KNOW.

AN EMPTY LIFE

WHY DOES LIFE LEAVE ME LIKE THIS?

SOMETIMES I THINK AND THEN INSIST.

THAT THINGS AREN'T ALWAYS THIS BAD

SOMETIMES I AM HAPPY THEN AGAIN, I'M SAD.

ABOUT THE MANY PROBLEMS THAT I HAVE IN STORE

IT MAKES ME THINK AND WANT NO MORE.

SUNSHINE ON MY LONG DARK DAYS

AND CHEER ME UP IN MANY WAYS.

WHY DOES LIFE MAKE ME FEEL REJECTED?

IT LEAVES ME ALONE AND UNDETECTED.

OF THE PROBLEMS OF MANY OTHERS

SOME ARE WEARY SISTERS, FATHERS, AND BROTHERS.

THAT HAVE SUFFERED HARDSHIPS AS WELL AS YOU

IN EVERYTHING THEY TRY TO DO.

WHY DOES LIFE LEAVE US IN DIFFERENT SITUATIONS?

THAT ARE CONFRONTED BY MANY PEOPLE IN DIFFERENT NATIONS.

NATIONS THAT ARE NEAR AND FAR

IT MAYBE PEACE THEN AGAIN, IT'S WAR.

WARS THAT LEAVE MANY CRYING

FOR CERTAIN OUR BROTHERS ARE REALLY DYING.

THINGS IN LIFE ARE LIKE A MERRY-GO-ROUND

IT KEEPS YOU IN THE AIR AND YOU NEVER TOUCH THE GROUND

LONELINESS

LONLINESS CREEPS IN LIKE THE WINTER SNOW
IT MAKES YOU WONDER AND IT MAKES YOU GO.
TO PLACES FAR BEYOND YOUR GOAL
IT LEAVES YOU WEARY AND LOOKING OLD.
TO ME LONLINESS IS NOT THE BEST
IT LEAVES YOU WORRIED AND THAT'S A MESS.
OF ALL THE PEOPLE IN THIS WORLD
LONLINESS TAKES THE PLACE OF ONE LITTLE GIRL.
ONE TOO YOUNG TO REALLY KNOW
BEFORE I WOULD BE LONELY, I WOULDN'T LET HER GO.
SHE LEFT MY HEART ACHING FOR WANT OF JOY
SHE PLAYED WITH LONLINESS LIKE IT WAS A TOY.
SOMETIMES I SIT AND THINK WITH A DOUBT
WILL SHE BRING BACK MY LOVE AND LET LONLINESS OUT?
IT SEEMS AS THOUGH SHE DOESN'T COMPREHEND
SO, I GUESS I'LL BE LONELY TO THE VERY END.
NOT KNOWING WHAT LIFE HAS IN STORE
I SHOULD FIND ANOTHER AND LET LONLINESS GO.
THERE IS NO ONE TO TAKE HER PLACE
SO, I WILL LIVE WITH LONLINESS AND DISGRACE.
I WOULD RATHER BE LONELY AND LOST
THAN TO FIND ANOTHER AND PAY THE COST.
OF BEING LONELY AGAIN AND AGAIN
BLOWING THROUGH LIFE LIKE THE SUMMER WIND.
BUT LONELINESS IS NOT BAD AT ALL
YOU MUST FIGHT THE BATTLE STANDING TALL.
FOR ONCE YOU LOSE STILL TROUBLE FREE
LONLINESS WILL GO THROUGH YOUR UFE ON A SHOPPING SPREE.

GATHERING EVERYTHING THAT WILL MAKE YOU SIN

IT WILL BELITTLE YOU AND TAKE A FRIEND.

TO A TREK INTO THE UNKNOWN

YOU MUST BE SMART AND ALSO STRONG.

AS A FAIR WARNING I MUST SAY

DO YOUR BEST TO KEEP LONLINESS AWAY.

LONLINESS CREEPS LIKE THE WINTER SNOW

LONLINESS CREEPS LIKE THE WINTER SNOW
AND CONSTANTLY HAUNTS WHEREVER YOU GO.
AGONY, GRIEF, AND PAIN CAPTURES YOUR SOUL
ALL OF THESE ARE CRUEL AND SO VERY COLD.
YOUR HEART BEATS WITH EXTREME STRESS
ANGUISH FROM YOUR STRUGGLE LEAVES YOU IN A MESS.
NO PLACE TO TURN OR DESTINATION
NOTHING TO SOOTHE AND NO CONSOLATION.
THE OUTSIDE WORLD WILL REMAIN WITH PATIENCE
AND THE SADDEST SONGS WILL BE YOUR CLOSET RELATION.
FOR LONLINESS KEEPS YOU ON THE GO
IT REALLY CREEPS IN LIKE THE WINTER SNOW.

CRYING TIME

IT'S CRYING TIME ONCE MORE
MY BABY LEFT ME FEELING LOW.
TOO LOW TO EVEN TO CRY
WHEN I LOOKED AT HER TO SAY GOODBYE.
GOODBYE UNTIL SHE CHANGES HER MIND
MY BABY'S GONE SO IT'S CRYING TIME.

IT'S CRYING TIME IT REALLY IS
WHEN SHE DEPARTED SO CAME THE TEARS.
TEARS THAT WERE SHED IN VAIN
SHE LEFT ME HURT AND FULL OF PAIN.
I DIDN'T HAVE TIME TO USE MY LINE
MY BABY'S GONE SO IT'S CRYING TIME.

IT'S CRYING TIME IT HAS TO BE
MY HEART IS TORN AND FANCY FREE.
WHEN I SEE THAT MY BABY'S GONE
IT BRINGS THE TEARS AND LEAVE ME ALONE.
I TRIED REAL HARD TO CHANGE HER MIND
MY BABY'S GONE SO IT'S CRYING TIME.

MOTHER' DAY

MOTHER'S DAY I WAS VERY DISAPPOINTED.
I WANTED TO GIVE MY MOTHER A PRESENT
BUT I COULDN'T GET WHAT SHE WANTED.
NEXT YEAR WILL NOT LEAVE ME LIKE THIS
IN ANY WAY, FORM OR FASHION.
I WILL GET HER THE PRESENT IF SHE INSIST
WITH LOVE, UNDERSTANDING AND PASSION.
SO, IF YOU REALLY KNOW YOUR MOTHER
WITHOUT ANY REASON OR DOUBT.
TRY TO GET HER WHAT SHE WANTS
BEFORE SHE BEGAN TO SHOUT.

CRYING

CYRING IS LIKE THE FALLING RAIN

YOUR TEARS WILL COMFORT YOU AND EASE THE PAIN.

SO, I CRY NOW WHEN I AM ALONE

JUST A WASTE OF TIME SITTING AT HOME.

I HAVE SHED MANY TEARS DURING MY LIFE

I SHED THE MOST OF THEM WHEN I LOST MY WIFE.

NOW I AM CRYING WHILE I AM HURTING

I WILL CRY AGAIN AND THAT IS FOR CERTAIN.

SOME DON'T UNDERSTAND WHY A MAN HAS TO CRY

AND SERIOUSLY SPEAKING THAT IS NO LIE.

I SAW MY BEST GIRL KISSING ANOTHER GUY

~ AND I TRIED TO HOLD BACK BUT I HAD TO CRY.

PEOPLE OFTEN CRY WHEN THEY LOSE A FRIEND

AND SOME WILL GRIEVE TO THE VERY END.

IF YOU HAVE TO CRY BE VERY PROUD

SHED THOSE TEARS AND DON'T BE LOUD.

DEATH

DEATH IS A DARK DAY IN YOUR LIFE

IT MIGHT TAKE YOUR HUSBAND OR YOUR WIFE.

LEAVING YOU CRYING WITH DEEP SORROW

DON'T CRY DARLING THERE IS A TOMORROW.

IF YOU COULD UNDERSTAND WHAT DEATH HAS DONE

IT MIGHT TAKE A DAUGHTER OR MAYBE A SON.

FOR DEATH IS TOUGH AND UNJUST

IT WILL LEAVE YOU CRYING AND THAT'S A MUST.

YOU REALLY CANNOT LIVE ALWAYS

DEATH WILL LEAVE SOME LONG DARK DAYS.

DAYS THAT ARE LONG AND SEEM NEVER TO END

DEATH WILL OVERTAKE A VERY CLOSE FRIEND.

FOR IT YOU MEET DEATH BE WILLING TO GIVE

YOU CAN STAY DEAD LONGER THAN YOU CAN LIVE.

ANOTHER DAY HAS GONE

ANOTHER DAY HAS GONE

AND I FEEL ALL ALONE.

I TALKED TO GOD ABOVE

TO TAKE CARE OF THE ONE I LOVE.

AS I CONTINUE TO PRAY

I ASK GOD TO GIVE ME ONE MORE DAY.

ONE DAY SO I CAN LIVE AGAIN

AND TRY TO BE A BETTER MAN.

JUST SITTING HERE AT HOME ALONE

I THANK GOD ANOTHER DAY HAS GONE.

THE VERDICT IS YOURS

THE VERDICT IS YOURS AND I MUST SAY
WHETHER I LIVE TOMORROW OR DIE TODAY.
I HAVE LIVED AND TRIED TO DO MY BEST
TO BE CONSIDERATE AND FIGHT LONELINESS.
BUT LONELINESS IS A PAIN
IT WILL MAKE YOU WEAK AND CRY IN VAIN.
THE TEARS YOU SHED MAY NOT HELP
BUT IT EASES YOUR MIND AND GIVES YOU PEP.
PEP TO KEEP YOU MOVING ON
YOU MAYBE RIGHT OR YOU CAN BE WRONG.
TO WANDER AMONG THE OCEAN SHORES
I SAY TO MYSELF THE VERDICT IS YOURS.

HAPPINESS

    HAPPINESS IS THE BEST THING IN LIFE
I GUESS YOU REALLY KNOW.
IT PUTS A GLOW INTO YOUR HEART
DURING RAIN, SHINE, SLEET OR SNOW.
PUTTING LONLINESS AND HATE
INTO A VERY SPECIAL PLACE.
AWAY GOES SORROW AND ALSO DISGRACE.
    BUT HAPPINESS IS SOMETIMES A THREAT
IT MAKES YOU WONDER AND OFTEN FORGET.
THAT ONE CANNOT BE HAPPY ALONE
FOR HAPPINESS SHOULD START IN THE HOME.
TO THE WEAK I MUST SAY
LET HAPPINESS DRIVE LONLINESS AWAY.
THEN YOU CAN SAY WITH A SMILE
AT LEAST I AM HAPPY FOR A WHILE.

PRAYING

PRAYING IS VERY HELPFUL IN MANY WAYS

IT WILL TAKE AWAY THE TENSIONS OF YOUR WORRIED DAYS.

A LITTLE PRAYER WILL HURT NO ONE

IT IS JUST LIKE TALKING AND HAVING LOTS OF FUN.

TALKING TO THE GOOD LORD ABOVE

THE ONE THAT EVERYONE SHOULD LOVE.

IF YOU DON'T HAVE TIME TO PRAY

HOW DO YOU EXPECT GOD TO HELP YOU TODAY?

A PRAYER DOES NOT HAVE TO BE LONG AND DRAWN OUT

YOU DON'T HAVE TO GO TO CHURCH OR TRY TO SHOUT.

TO GET THE LORD TO EASE THE TENSION

WHENEVER YOU GO GIVE PART OF YOUR PENSION.

PLEASE DON'T FORGET WHAT I HAVE SAID

A LITTLE PRAYER WILL YOU GET AHEAD.

A PRAYER IS CERTAINLY NOT A SIN

IT WILL BE WITH YOU TO THE VERY END.

IF YOU LOSE FAITH AND DON'T HAVE TIME

LET A LITLE PRAYER CHANGE YOUR MIND.

DRIVING

IF YOU ARE DRIVING
DON'T BE LIKE JOHN DOE.
HE GOT KILLED NOT SLIDING
BUT DRIVING AWFUL SLOW.

IT'S LOTS OF FUN RIDING
AND HAVING A GOOD TIME.
STOP TEXTING WHILE DRIVING
AND DRINKING LOTS OF WINE.

MARY JANE GOT KILLED ONE DAY
WHILE GOING TO SEE A FRIEND.
SHE THOUGHT SHE HAD THE RIGHT-OF-WAY
BUT IT WAS DEATH TO THE VERY END.

DRIVE SAFE AS YOU CAN
CAUTION AND AT THE RIGHT SPEED.
WATCH OUT FOR THE OTHER MAN
FOLLOW ALL SIGNS AND PLEASE TAKE HEED.

WHAT SHOULD I DO?

VALENTINE'S DAY IS ONLY A FEW HOURS AWAY

I AM JUST SITTING HERE THINKING ABOUT WHAT I MUST SAY.

TO A GIRL THAT I LOVE SO VERY TRUE

GEE, I AM PUZZLED AND DON'T KNOW WHAT TO DO.

I COULD TELL HER THAT I LOVE HER IN MANY SITUATIONS

BUT THESE ARE TERMS USED IN MANY NATIONS.

I COULD GIVE HER THE LOVE OF A CHILD

BUT SHE WOULD ONLY LOOK AT ME WITH A SMILE.

I SHOULD TELL HER THAT I LOVE HER AS A FRIEND

AND I'LL ALWAYS LOVE HER TO THE VERY END.

SOMEONE PLEASE HELP ME MAKE UP MY MIND

FOR TIME IS SURELY FLYING.

I AM REALLY CONFUSED AS I CAN BE

SOMEONE PLEASE SIT DOWN AND HELP ME.

I LOVE MY GIRL WITH ALL MY HEART

SHE IS A WONDERFUL GIRL AND VERY SMART.

PLEASE SEND YOUR THOUGHTS AS SOON AS YOU CAN

FOR I NEED HELP NOW AND I'LL UNDERSTAND.

IF I COULD JUST CLIMB THIS FENCE

WHEN I WAS YOUNG AND VERY ENERGETIC

I WANTED TO PLAY BALL BUT I HAD TO FORGET IT.

I HAD A LOT OF FAITH AND CONFIDENCE.

I KNEW THAT I WOULD GET TO PLAY

IF I COULD JUST CLIMB THIS FENCE.

THIS FENCE WAS AROUND THE PLAYGROUND

IT WAS VERY TALL AND A RUSTY BROWN.

SCHOOL CLOSED; I HAVEN'T PLAYED SINCE

I WOULD PLAY TODAY IF I COULD JUST CLIMB THIS FENCE.

MY TEACHER

MY TEACHER DOES SO MANY THINGS
SHE HAS A HEART OF GOLD.
SHE HAS A SMILE SO WARM AND TENDER
IN A ROOM THAT IS SOMETIMES COLD.
SHE LEADS A LIFE OF TEACHING KIDS
MANY THANKLESS TASKS.
SHE IS SOMEONE THAT TEACHS HARD
BUT VERY SELDOM ASK.
IT MEANS THAT VERY SOMEONE THAT
IS NOT A MINISTER OR A PREACHER.
I CAN SAY IT IN ONE SIMPLE PHRASE
ONLY YOU, ONLY YOU ....MY TEACHER.

ONCE I WAS A SLAVE

ONCE I WAS A SLAVE IN THE OLD WORLD

I HAD THREE BOYS AND ONE LITTLE GIRL

WE HAD TO SURVIVE FROM THE FAT OF THE LAND

I HAD BLISTERS ON MY FEET AND CUTS ON MY HAND.

MY MASTER WAS A MAN FULL OF HATE

HE WOULD MAKE YOU SUFFER AND OFTEN WAIT.

FOR THE NEXT DAY TO COME WITH SORROW AND SWEAT

HE WOULD MAKE YOU SUFFER AND OFTEN FORGET.

THAT ONCE YOU WERE DOING THE BEST YOU CAN

TO BE HAPPY IN THIS FOREIGN LAND.

AFTER WORK HE WOULD TIE US TO A TREE

AND MAKE US FORGET THAT ONCE WE WERE FREE.

ONE DAY FROM THE NORTH CAME A BIG THUNDER

WE WERE SET FREE AND BEGAN TO WONDER.

WHETHER OUR DREAM HAS COME TRUE

THE SKY WAS FULL OF HOPE AND WE WERE TOO.

FOR ONCE AGAIN I AM A MAN

TO FORGET IF I ONLY CAN.

THAT THE DAYS WERE DARK AND GRAVE

FOR ONCE IN MY LIFE, I WAS A SLAVE.

A HARD STRUGGLE

IT'S BEEN A HARD STRUGGGLE FOR MY RACE
FOR SOCIETY HAS HELD US BACK.
THEY HAVE EVEN STEPPED UP THE PACE
AND MADE US REALIZE THAT WE ARE BLACK.
OUR PEOPLE HAVE TRIED FOR MANY YEARS TO GET THEIR CIVIL RIGHTS
IN WHATEVER THE HAVE TRIED TO DO.
THEY HAVE HAD SOME WORRIED DAYS AND LONG HARD NIGHTS
SO MUCH OF THIS IS TRUE.
MARTIN LUTHER KING WAS KILLED ONE DAY
WHILE DOING THE BEST HE COULD.
HIS MURDERER HAS TO PAY
IF THINGS ARE LIKE THEY SHOULD.
JOHN AND HIS BROTHER WERE KILLED
WHILE FIGHTING FOR OUR CAUSE.
THEY TRIED TO HELP US BUILD
BUT NOW IT IS JUST A PAUSE.
I HOPE THAT PEOPLE WILL REALIZE
WHAT SOCIETY HAS DONE.
BY TELLING US LIES AND ALIBIS
WE WOULD RATHER FIGHT THAN RUN.

FATE

WHEN THINGS SEEM SO UNCERTAIN
AND PEOPLE ARE FULL OF HATE.
LIFE SEEMS TO HAVE ITS HIGHS AND LOWS
SOME SAY THAT THIS IS FATE.
TIMES ARE HARD AND FRIENDS ARE FEW
I GUESS SOME OF YOU MUST KNOW.
MAY NO FATE PRE-DETERMINE ME
BUT KEEP ME ON THE GO.
FOR THOSE THAT DON'T UNDERSTAND
DON'T THINK THAT IT IS TOO LATE.
BELIEVE ME DESTINY IS INESCAPABLE
FOR IT IS CERTAINLY THE SAME AS FATE.

I WONDER

TO PAST GENERATIONS THAT HAVE SURRENDERED TO THE FAILURES OF LIFE.
MY GOAL IN LIFE IS TO INCORPORATE LOVING AND UNDERSTANDING OF
MY APTITUDE AND MY ALTITUDE AS MY MIND GATHERS THE TWO AS ONE.
ONLY WHERE LIFE, LOVING AND FORGIVING ARE SOLIDIFIED.
THE TEACHINGS ARE DIFFERENT AND THE MORALS ARE THE SAME.
IS LIFE EVER JUSTIFIED FOR THOSE WHO PLAY THE GAME?
I WONDER..........

A CHILD'S PRAYER

DEAR LORD AS I PRAY TO YOU

AS EVERY BOY AND GIRL SHOULD DO.

I ASK YOU TO MAKE THIS A BETTER WORLD

FOR ANY GROWING BOY OR GIRL.

TAKE AWAY ALL THE HARDSHIPS THAT

MY PARENTS WILL HAVE TO FACE.

MAKE THINGS SO VERY EASY

SO THAT WE CAN GO ANY PLACE.

TELL ALL THE DIFFERENT PEOPLE

NOT TO BREAK THE CABLE

DO AWAY WITH ALL THE FIGHTING

AND BRING FOLKS TO THE TABLE.

I END MY PRAYER DEAR LORD BY SAYING

I WILL NOT GET AN ANSWER IF I STOP PRAYING.

AND IF I SHOULD DIE BEFORE I WAKE

I HOPE TO SEE YOU AT THOSE HEAVENLY GATES.

UNDERSTANDING

JUST THE OTHER DAY I HEARD A MAN SAY

AND HE WASN'T A MINISTER OR A PREACHER.

HE TALKED TO HIS DAUGHTER IN SUCH A WAY

UNDERSTANDING WAS THE BEST TEACHER.

UNDERSTANDING IS A VERY ODD BAG

TO MANY THAT REALLY DON'T KNOW.

IT IS SOMETHING THAT WILL NOT LET YOU BRAG

BUT KEEP YOU ON THE GO.

TO GREATER GOALS IN THIS WORLD

WITH DIFFERENT PLACES IN MIND.

WHETHER YOU ARE A BOY OR GIRL

OR JUST WASTING TIME.

IT IS NOT VERY DEMANDING

AND IT IS REALLY NOT ANY JIVE.

YOU CAN'T BEAT UNDERSTANDING

IF YOU HAVE THE DESIRE TO SURVIVE.

TO THE PEOPLE

SOME PEOPLE ARE VERY DEMANDING
AND SOME ARE VERY SLOW.
SOME HAVE THAT UNDERSTANDING
WITH PLACES IN MIND TO GO.
OTHERS ARE DUMB TO THE FACT
WITHOUT A GOAL IN MIND.
YOU CAN TELL BY THE WAY THEY ACT
THEY ARE NOT FAMILIAR WITH MANKIND.
I MET A MAN THE OTHER DAY
THAT WAS TRYING HARD TO SURVIVE.
HE ACTED IN SUCH A STRANGE WAY
I THOUGHT HE WAS FULL OF LIES.
PEOPLE SHOULD TRY TO REALIZE
IN EVERYTHING THEY DO.
DON'T TELL LIES AND ALIBIS
ONLY TRY TO BE JUST YOU.

I AM IN A DIFFERENT WORLD

ONE STEP BACK INTO A DEPTH OF NO RETURN

NEVER TO COME BACK FOR IT IS THE END.

NO MATTER HOW LONG I YEARN

FOR THE LOST OF A DEAR FRIEND.

THAT HAS BEEN WITH ME ALL ALONG

WHILE I AM SITTING HERE AT HOME ALONE.

THINKING ABOUT THAT CLOSE FRIEND

THAT I LOVED SO VERY DEAR.

FOR IT IS THE BEGINNING OF THE END

I AM FULL OF TEARS AND FEAR.

I AM IN A DIFFERENT WORLD

WHETHER I AM FAR OR NEAR.

JESUS GIVE ME ONE MORE DAY

JESUS GIVE ME ONE MORE DAY

LORD I NEED JUST ONE MORE DAY

JESUS GIVE ME ONE MORE DAY

AND I'LL BE ON MY WAY.

CHARIOTS ARE FLYING THROUGH THE SKY

PEOPLE ARE SINGING BY AND BY

LORD I NEED JUST ONE MORE DAY

AND I'LL BE ON MY WAY.

IF YOU THINK THAT YOU HAVE SINNED

TALK TO JESUS HE'S YOUR FRIEND.

LORD I NEED JUST ONE MORE DAY

AND I'LL BE ON MY WAY.

WHEN SATAN TRYS TO ATTACK

YOU DON'T WORRY JESUS HAS YOUR BACK.

LORD, I NEED JUST ONE MORE DAY

AND I'LL BE ON MY WAY.

www.ingramcontent.com/pod-product-compliance
Lightning Source LLC
Chambersburg PA
CBHW072028040426
42447CB00009B/1776